Women in War

BY REBECCA RISSMAN

CONTENT CONSULTANT
Amelia F. Underwood
Adjunct Professor, Department of Military Science
James Madison University

Essential Library

An Imprint of Abdo Publishing | abdopublishing.com

WOMEN'S LIVES *in* *History*

abdopublishing.com

Published by Abdo Publishing, a division of ABDO, PO Box 398166, Minneapolis, Minnesota 55439. Copyright © 2017 by Abdo Consulting Group, Inc. International copyrights reserved in all countries. No part of this book may be reproduced in any form without written permission from the publisher. Essential Library™ is a trademark and logo of Abdo Publishing.

Printed in the United States of America, North Mankato, Minnesota
042016
092016

THIS BOOK CONTAINS RECYCLED MATERIALS

Cover Photo: Shutterstock Images; iStockphoto
Interior Photos: US National Archives and Records Administration, 4–5, 6, 38; US Air Force, 8, 82–83, 88–89; US Army, 10–11, 62, 87; Carol M. Highsmith Archive/Library of Congress, 13; Everett Historical/Shutterstock Images, 14–15, 17, 19, 28–29, 32; Bain News Service/Library of Congress, 21; Howard Chandler Christy/Library of Congress, 24; US Army Signal Corps, 26, 27; AP Images, 30, 52, 59, 74; Al Aumuller/Library of Congress, 34; Life/AP Images, 36; Adam CC2.0, 40–41; Hulton Archive/Getty Images, 43; Joseph McKeown/Picture Post/Getty Images, 44–45; National Security Agency, 47; US Marine Corps, 48–49, 79; Genevieve Naylor/Corbis, 54; US Department of Defense, 55, 69, 96; Wisconsin Historical Society, WHS–86868, 56–57; US Military Academy, 65; Bettmann/Corbis, 66–67; Gerard Fouet/Getty Images, 70; Julie Jacobson/AP Images, 76–77; Joe Paydock/Kent State Army ROTC, 85; US Navy, 90; John Bazemore/AP Images, 92; Jessica McGowan/Getty Images, 94–95

Editor: Megan Anderson
Series Designer: Maggie Villaume

Cataloging-in-Publication Data
Names: Rissman, Rebecca, author.
Title: Women in war / by Rebecca Rissman.
Description: Minneapolis, MN : Abdo Publishing, [2017] | Series: Women's lives in history | Includes bibliographical references and index.
Identifiers: LCCN 2015960326 | ISBN 9781680782967 (lib. bdg.) | ISBN 9781680774900 (ebook)
Subjects: LCSH: Women and war--Juvenile literature. | Women in the professions--Juvenile literature.
Classification: DDC 940--dc23
LC record available at http://lccn.loc.gov/2015960318

Contents

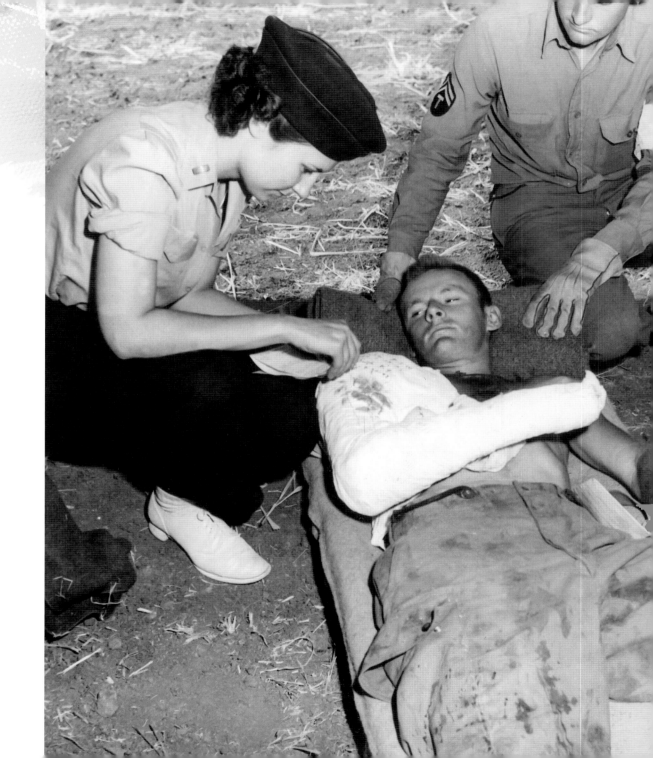

Nurse Verona Savinski tends to a wounded soldier during the 1944 invasion of Europe in World War II.

CHAPTER ONE

Females Who Fight

In 1943, US Army Air Corps nurse Elsie Ott arrived at a desert field hospital in Karachi, India, now Pakistan. World War II (1939–1945) was underway. American troops at the hospital had suffered terrible losses at the hands of the fierce Japanese military. Ott joined the army in 1941, but had little experience in handling the casualties of war. She was immediately overwhelmed by the sick and injured troops who badly needed her help.

Troops and their medical staff faced harsh conditions in many places in India. Intense weather, rough terrain, and poor roads meant evacuating sick patients could take weeks. In some cases, injured or sick soldiers were strapped to mules for the long journey to get medical care. Military leaders knew this was not the best way to evacuate their soldiers. Soon, they began flying sick patients out on military planes. This meant soldiers could be transported from bloody battlefields to surgery in only hours, rather than days or even weeks.

become a Nurse
YOUR COUNTRY NEEDS YOU
Write Nursing Information Bureau, 1790 Broadway, New York City

Nursing was just one of the many important roles women played in World War II.

Special Flight Mission

In January 1943, Ott was selected for an experimental medical flight. It was to fly approximately 10,000 miles (16,000 km) in seven days, dropping off and picking up patients around the world. Although Ott agreed to the mission, there were a few small problems. First, Ott had never flown on an airplane. Second, Ott would be the only nurse on board. Third, the plane had no medical equipment. Finally, the flight was expected to depart within hours. Immediately after receiving her assignment, Ott got to work, stocking the plane with medical supplies, mattresses, and anything else she could think of.

Despite the challenges she faced, Ott performed astoundingly well. She remained brave, even while flying in and out of dangerous war zones and over dangerous terrain. She provided nonstop care, even while the plane refueled. She communicated with doctors on the ground about the condition and needs of patients who were being dropped off or picked up. She even used her own money to pay for her patients' meals while on the ground. When the flight finally arrived in the United States, Ott helped carry patients off the plane and into the hospital as quickly as possible.

Military Recognition

Ott's courageous and efficient performance made a huge splash among military officials. She was the first woman ever awarded the Air Medal, a great honor. Her notes from this historic flight have shaped how air rescues operate today. She recommended that medical records be provided with the patients being evacuated. She also noted planes should be equipped with oxygen for patients in case of emergency. One of Ott's recommendations was specifically directed at women in her field—she objected to the uniforms nurses wore at the time. She suggested uniforms include slacks, rather than a skirt, to make patient care easier.

Ott was not the first woman to be called a wartime hero. Throughout history, women have

MARGARET CORBIN

Margaret Corbin fought alongside her husband, John, during the American Revolutionary War (1775–1783). On November 16, 1776, during an attack on Fort Washington on Manhattan Island, she handled ammunition while John stood at a cannon. When John was fatally wounded, Margaret took his place handling the cannon. She was eventually wounded herself and taken to Fort Lee in New Jersey to be treated. In 1779, the Supreme Executive Council of Pennsylvania recommended to the Board of War that Margaret receive a pension. Congress authorized that she receive half of a soldier's monthly pay for the rest of her life.

Ott became the first woman to receive the Air Medal.

been instrumental both on and off the battlefield. Whether working tirelessly on the home front, fighting at the front, or sneaking behind enemy lines, they have always had a place in war. However, not everyone has welcomed them.

Fighting for a Place in the Armed Forces

Women warriors have long had to battle social hurdles to participate in the armed forces. Sexism is a type of discrimination based on the belief that women are inferior to men. Sexism has historically played a large part in making it difficult for women to be involved in the armed forces, and it continues to affect their roles today.

Women who want to join the armed forces are often told they not as physically fit as men. This is reflected throughout history. Women were not allowed to work in physically strenuous occupations or participate in sporting events. Today, this idea is still present in the debate about a woman's role in the military.

Opponents argue women cannot complete the same physical tasks as men, such as lifting heavy loads. Because women are often smaller than men, their muscles are smaller. This logic is used to argue they are unfit to be on the battlefield. Critics claim this presents hazards not only to female soldiers, but to their male comrades as well. If, for example, a large, heavy soldier is wounded in battle, comrades must carry him or her to safety. Critics wonder whether a female soldier would be up to the task.

JOAN OF ARC

Joan of Arc is one of history's most famous female warriors. As a young girl, she approached the French army and volunteered to help in their fight against the English. Joan of Arc soon proved herself to be a serious fighter. In 1429, at age 17, she was a commander in the French army and led forces to victory over the English in Orléans, France. She was greatly respected for her understanding of military strategy. However, in 1430, the English captured her. The following year she was burned at the stake.

Critics also question a woman's emotional capacity to handle the stress, danger, and violence that comes with being in the military. This argument has a long history. In World War I (1914–1918), women were not allowed to fight. Not only that, but men were advised not to include too many disturbing details in letters to their wives and mothers back home. Many believed women could not handle such information. Recent politicians have also expressed doubts about a woman's emotional capacity to handle war. Former US senator and Republican presidential candidate Rick Santorum expressed concerns about women in combat in 2012. Santorum cited concerns about the "types of emotions involved" when women go to war.[1]

A Brotherhood Interrupted

Some people believe women negatively change the dynamic of war, arguing the "brotherhood" of soldiers is sacred and should not be disturbed by women. The logistics of a troop of male soldiers traveling, sleeping, bathing, and eating together could be complicated by the addition of women. Politician, Vietnam War (1955–1975) veteran, and former Secretary of the Navy Jim Webb said,

> Men fight better without women around. Men treat women differently than they do men, and vice versa. . . . These tendencies can be controlled in an eight-hour workday, but cannot be suppressed in a 24-hour, seven-days-a-week combat situation. Introducing women into combat units would greatly confuse an already confusing environment.[2]

The notion of brotherhood—absent of women—as an essential and bonding component of war is not new. In fact, playwright William Shakespeare coined the phrase "band of brothers" to

LOZEN

In the late 1800s, settlers in New Mexico forced an Apache tribe to live on a reservation. The conditions there were terrible, and soon the Apache revolted. A female warrior named Lozen rode alongside the men from her tribe as they raided the nearby land. She fought victoriously to defend her tribe. But she was also merciful. She worked to save women and children from the dangers of these battles. Later, Lozen joined the famous Apache warrior Geronimo as he fought against the US Army. Lozen's brother Chief Victorio described her admirably, saying she was "strong as a man, braver than most, and cunning in strategy. Lozen is a shield to her people."[5]

refer to the bond formed between male soldiers during war in his play *Henry V*.[3]

Roles for Women

Not all women want to serve in combat. Some are interested in other military positions, such as administrative work or positions in intelligence, communications, and transportation. As a path toward these roles, many women attend military academic institutions. Women have faced barricades to some of the United States' most elite military schools. In 1979, Webb commented on the issue, noting his belief that, "There is a place for women in our military, but not in combat. And their presence at institutions dedicated to the preparation of men for combat command is poisoning that preparation."[4]

Despite the often-overwhelming opposition, women in all five branches of the US military have performed heroically. Women have risen to elite ranks in the Army, Navy, Coast Guard, Air Force, and Marine Corps. They have been instrumental in the growth and success of each of these branches in times of both war and peace. Some of the female heroes of the US military worked in secret, without the knowledge of their fellow soldiers. Others worked on the front lines with the full support of their

The Women in the Military Service for America Memorial at Arlington National Cemetery in Virginia honors the service of women in military.

fellow troops. Women have played a fascinating role in the history of the armed forces, and will undoubtedly help shape its future.

WHY FIGHT?

Many people wonder why women choose to join the military. After all, war and military life is tough, dangerous, and stressful. During wartime, it often involves life and death scenarios. Political news correspondent Tucker Carlson once tweeted, "Feminism's latest victory: the right to get your limbs blown off in war. Congratulations."[6] Many female soldiers have argued they have the right to fight for their nation and serve in a military they love like their male counterparts do.

After World War I broke out, women supported the war effort by working in places such as shipyards.

CHAPTER TWO

The Great War

O n June 28, 1914, Sophie Chotek, Duchess von Hohenberg, was dressed in a beautiful white dress and veiled hat. She and her husband, Franz Ferdinand, the heir to the Austrian throne, were touring Sarajevo, Bosnia. During the tour, a man rushed the car and shot both Franz and Sophie dead.

The assassination sparked an international conflict that would soon come to be known as the Great War, and later as World War I. Austro-Hungarian leaders were outraged after learning about the assassination. They declared war on Bosnia. Germany, which was allied with Austria-Hungary, also declared war. Bosnia's allies rallied to support the nation. The conflict soon involved all of the great powers in Europe. Within weeks, Germany, Italy, and Austria-Hungary were at war with the United Kingdom, France, and Russia.

World War I ultimately involved 27 nations and their colonies around the world. It was an especially bloody war. Soldiers huddled in trenches for weeks and months, lobbing bombs, firing guns, and throwing poison gas into enemy trenches. More than 9 million men died during this conflict, and millions more were wounded.[1] But men were not alone in this fight. Women also played crucial roles in the war.

Helping on the Home Front

As millions of men left home to fight in the war, women around the world rallied to support their nations' military efforts. They were left behind to raise the children, earn money, and keep the economies of their home countries afloat.

Before World War I, women in many countries performed primarily domestic work and raised children. Women in the upper classes rarely worked outside the home. Women in lower socioeconomic classes worked, but they were limited to occupations considered appropriate for women, such as teaching, nursing, and administrative or secretarial jobs.

When war erupted, women were thrust into new social, economic, and political roles. Early attitudes toward the war told women to keep their homes ready and neat for their husbands. The popular 1914 song, "Keep the Home-fires Burning," reminded women their sons and husbands missed them and would soon be home. However, that changed as the war escalated. The war effort needed women, and it needed them immediately. Women began to assume more and more civilian roles on the home front. They took on odd jobs, worked in restaurants and shops, and labored in factories to supply arms and munitions to their troops—all while juggling home life and caretaking responsibilities.

Caring for the Wounded

Prior to World War I, thousands of women served as nurses during the American Civil War (1861–1865). When World War I started, women were once again thrust into the war effort in support and medical roles. Nursing was one of the most important contributions women made. Women around the world rushed to become trained as nurses so they could help treat the wounded soldiers who returned from battle. Many civilian organizations, such as the Red Cross, supported these efforts.

Nursing also opened an important door for women seeking active roles in armed forces around the world. In many cases, this was the first time women were openly welcomed into the military. The overwhelming need for medical support eroded the reservations military leaders

Women worked in munitions factories to create supplies needed for the war effort.

previously had about women's capabilities of serving bravely near battle.

British Women

At the war's outset, British women were discouraged from participating in most wartime activities. A doctor named Elsie Inglis watched the men in her community leave to join the fight. She wanted to help, too. When she offered to start a women's ambulance unit, a military officer responded, "My good lady, go home and sit still!"[2]

With their husbands gone, British women farmed, operated businesses, and earned money for their families. They also trained in support roles, such as nursing, to help their country's military remain as strong as possible.

Before the war began, the main group of British military nurses was the Queen Alexandra's Imperial Military Nursing Service, and it numbered only approximately 300 women. By the end of the

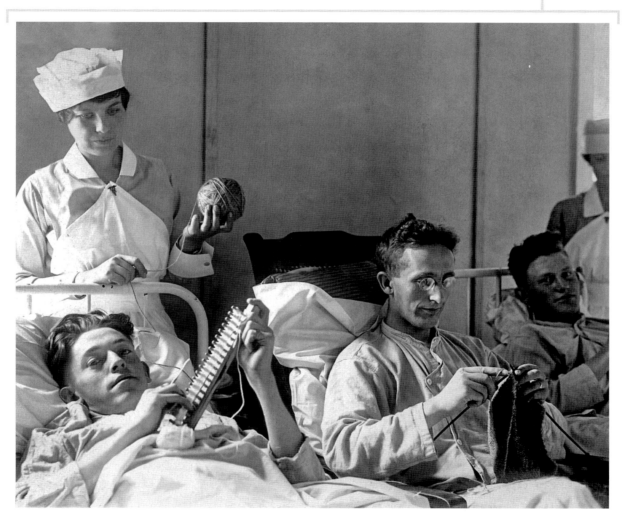

Nurses assist wounded World
War I soldiers with knitting at Walter
Reed Hospital in Washington, DC.

war, it accounted for more than 10,000 nurses.[5] These military nurses were trained professionals and worked tirelessly to care for victims of the war.

Although most nurses were kept safe behind the lines of battle, not all were willing to remain so far from the action. Elsie Knocker and Mairi Chisholm were two British nurses who worked directly on the front lines. They set up a first-aid post on the Belgian front line, where they saved many lives treating soldiers. Each woman was awarded 17 medals by the end of the war.

The British military also opened up more roles for women. In 1917, the Women's Auxiliary Army Corps (WAAC) was formed. This military organization allowed women to serve as chauffeurs, clerks, instructors, and other occupations that had been filled by men. The success of the WAAC led the British military to form the Women's Royal Air Force (WRAF) the following year. The WRAF employed women as drivers, cooks, storekeepers, clerks, and other important jobs. In total, more than 100,000 British women served essential roles in the military during World War I.[6]

Russian Women

Like women in the United Kingdom, Russian women helped out on the home front, running stores and working in munitions factories. They also served as nurses in the Sisters of Mercy of the Russian Red Cross.

Some Russian women wanted to fight. Russian law technically forbade women from joining combat, so some women disguised themselves as men. Others fought openly as women, either relying on close relationships with commanding officers or believing authorities would not punish them.

In 1917, word about individual women infiltrating male units spread throughout the Russian military. National urgency amongst the Russian people to end the war inspired women to beg the government to allow women to fight openly in the military. The secretary of war allowed a peasant named Maria Bochkareva to command the first Russian Women's Battalion of Death. The Women's Battalion initially numbered approximately 2,000 women, but only approximately 250 went into actual combat.[7] They were deployed to a battle near present day Smarhon, Belarus. Some women hid in the trenches, while others fought valiantly and even charged toward the front while their male comrades wanted to pull back.

Maria Bochkareva commanded her unit with strict discipline.

Their charge failed and they were eventually forced to retreat. Despite the defeat, the group was effective in shaming some Russian men who considered deserting from the armed services. If women could fight, the logic went, then men could fight, too. But the group did not succeed in revitalizing a weary Russian army.

French Female Fighters

Women in France played an important role in World War I. They fulfilled important duties on the home front, such as family caretaking. They also worked in munitions factories, creating and assembling vital supplies needed for war, such as guns, bullets, and bombs. In addition to these tasks, French women took on daring combat and espionage roles.

Emilinne Moreau was only 16 years old when she risked her life for the sake of her country. After Germans attacked her home, she saw Scottish soldiers heading toward the Germans. She ran to the Scottish soldiers and frantically warned them to change their route. Then she assisted the Scottish soldiers, who transformed her home into a makeshift first aid station for wounded troops. But

Moreau's involvement didn't stop there. Spotting a group of German soldiers preparing to shoot a wounded Scottish soldier, Moreau killed them with a grenade. Soon after this incident, Moreau was caring for an injured soldier in her home when a bullet whizzed past her head. Enraged, she reached for a male nurse's gun and killed two German soldiers.

The French and British governments bestowed several awards upon Moreau. She became a symbol of the French-British alliance and of the strength and force of women on the home front.

Louise de Bettignies was another fierce French fighter. Unlike Moreau, who fought openly, Bettignies served the French secretly. She became a spy for the French, British, and Belgian governments. Bettignies carried messages to the British government about the location of German troops. The German government was constantly on the lookout for spies, so this was extremely dangerous work. In 1916, she was captured and interrogated. In 1918, she died in a German prison camp. After her death, she was awarded the War Cross and Legion of Honour, two French military decorations.

American Women in World War I

The United States was hesitant to join the war at first. On May 7, 1915,

WAR RELIEF SERVICES

Not all women who served the United States did so as part of the armed services. Many volunteered with organizations such as the Red Cross and the Salvation Army. These groups operated both in the United States and abroad to equip troops with essential wartime supplies, such as bandages and food. Female volunteers traveled directly to the soldiers most in need, serving coffee and donuts in military camps and helping soldiers write letters home.

I WANT YOU

for THE NAVY

PROMOTION FOR ANY ONE ENLISTING
APPLY ANY RECRUITING STATION
OR POSTMASTER

The US government used posters to encourage women to enlist as yeomen (F).

a German U-boat, or submarine, sank the *Lusitania,* a British passenger ship carrying many Americans. American support for entering the war increased following this event and additional attacks on American freight ships. In 1917, the United States finally entered the war.

World War I was full of firsts for women in the US armed services. It was the first time women were allowed to enlist in the military in non-nursing roles. It was also the first time navy and army nurses were permitted to serve overseas.

More than 11,000 women joined the US Navy at a rank of yeoman (F).[8] Most of these women worked in clerical jobs as secretaries, administrators, and telephone operators. Some also held more traditionally male jobs, such as truck drivers, mechanics, and cryptographers. They provided assistance essential to the war effort, but the idea that women were inferior to men was still rampant throughout the US armed services. Women earned much less than men in the same roles and were also often denied promotion to management positions. Their job titles reflected this inequality. For example, female telephone operators, whose work was essential to the war effort, were referred to as "Hello Girls."

American women served bravely and valiantly during the war, despite often being in grave danger. More than 350 American servicewomen died during this war, many from a worldwide outbreak of influenza.[9]

When the war ended in 1918, people around the globe were left to deal with its aftermath. The massive scale of the war not only changed the political and cultural climate for everyone involved, but it had a special effect on women. They had experienced new freedoms and responsibilities. After the Great War, many women looked to the future and hoped for new opportunities for greatness.

Hello *Girls*

During World War I, the US Army sent more than 400 women overseas to serve as telephone operators in the United Kingdom and France.[10] Most of these women were fluent in both French and English, and they received extensive training in military radio communications. Known as the "Hello Girls," these women performed crucial wartime work by helping to ease communication between American, British, and French fighters.

The Hello Girls weren't recognized for their service in World War I until 1978.

When the first unit of Hello Girls deployed, dense fog left their ferry stranded in the English Channel. This was an incredibly dangerous predicament. At the time, Germany had been sinking approximately 25 percent of the British vessels offshore. The telephone operators were forced to remain on deck for two days, ready to abandon ship at a moment's notice. Commanding Officer Grace Banker later remembered how her unit remained in good spirits despite the

The Hello Girls run the telephones
in barracks in Tours, France.

frightening situation. "What good sports the girls were in the First Unit!" Banker said. "They took everything in their stride."[11]

These women were sworn into service, wore army uniforms, and served in a unit known as the Signal Corps Female Telephone Operators Unit 25. But at the end of the war, these women were denied veteran status. In 1978, President Jimmy Carter finally recognized their service when he signed a bill giving them veteran status.

Three US battleships burn after the attack on Pearl Harbor.

CHAPTER THREE

Women in World War II

On December 7, 1941, First Lieutenant Annie Fox was on duty as chief nurse at Hickman Field at Pearl Harbor, a US naval base on Oahu Island, Hawaii. Japanese warplanes appeared in the air above the base, shocking Americans by dropping bombs onto US battleships, planes, and buildings. As the base burned, troops and civilians on the ground raced to save those trapped in the flames. The United States had just been plunged into war.

As chaos engulfed Pearl Harbor, Fox remained calm. She quickly got to work, caring for injured soldiers and civilians. Even in the middle of the bombardment, when many other nurses feared for their own lives, Fox was focused on the well-being of her patients. She treated people with severe burns and injuries and helped to administer anesthesia. Her focus and bravery was so outstanding she became the first woman in US history to earn a military honor known as a Purple Heart. Two years later, the criteria

Fox enlisted during World War I and was a 23-year US Army veteran when the Japanese attacked Pearl Harbor in 1941.

for earning a Purple Heart changed to those who were wounded or killed in military action. Fox was then awarded a Bronze Star in place of her Purple Heart.

Roles between Wars

In the years between World War I and World War II, much of life returned to the way it was in the beginning of the century. Most women left their jobs and returned home and most men resumed their former careers.

However, women had made lasting social, economic, and political progress during World War I. Some women maintained their wartime careers, in both military and civilian roles. The contributions women made in the war supported the suffrage movement, which fought to give women the right to vote. Women earned the right to vote in the United States after

Congress passed the Nineteenth Amendment in 1920. That same year, the army changed its policy to allow nurses to achieve new ranks, from second lieutenant all the way up to major. Americans recognized the role of women was slowly changing.

The World at War, Again

Japan's attack on Pearl Harbor marked the US entrance into World War II, which started in 1939. The totalitarian leaders of Germany, Italy, and Japan were clamoring for domination over neighboring nations. These three countries became known as the Axis powers. They opposed the Allies, which chiefly consisted of France, the United Kingdom, and China. The Soviet Union joined the Allies in June 1941, and the United States followed in December 1941.

In 1939, Germany took the first step in sparking the war by invading neighboring Poland. Not long after, the United Kingdom, France, and the Soviet Union became involved in the conflict. By the time the war ended in 1945, more than 50 nations and 70 million people were involved in the fighting.[1]

ROSIE THE RIVETER

During the war, nearly 37 percent of the American workforce was female.[2] The US government created the character of Rosie the Riveter as propaganda. Wearing a bandana and flexing her arm with her sleeves rolled up, Rosie the Riveter encouraged women to work, even in jobs previously held only by men. Two of the biggest fields women worked in during the war were aviation and munitions. Building planes and weapons were jobs that would have been considered inappropriate for women in the years before the war. But they were essential to the war effort. Rosie the Riveter helped convince women to take on positions in these fields. Although women were needed, their work was not recognized. Women earned only approximately 50 percent as much as their male counterparts earned at their wartime jobs.[3]

Women learned skills such as welding to help with the war effort.

As they did during World War I, women on the home front quickly stepped into roles traditionally held by men. They drove buses, ran restaurants, labored on farms, and sailed fishing boats. They worked in factories to provide the military with weapons, supplies, and vehicles.

Women on the home front also helped their country by growing gardens of fruits and vegetables to reduce the strain on the country's agricultural system. They saved as many resources as possible for soldiers who needed them. They patched and reused old clothing and rationed gas, metal, and rubber.

Women Go to War

Many US military leaders, including General George C. Marshall, wanted to use women in different capacities during the war. In May 1942, the WAAC was formed. This branch of the army used women in noncombat positions both at home and abroad. Marshall also appointed Oveta Culp Hobby as the first director of the WAAC. Hobby was charged with finding jobs women could do with very little training.

More than 350,000 women served during World War II.[4] In addition to the WAAC (later known as the Women's Army Corps, or WAC), the US military quickly organized other new units for women. The navy formed the Women's Navy Reserves, called WAVES. The Coast Guard created SPARS, an acronym for the Coast Guard motto, "Semper Paratus—Always Ready."[5] The army created the Women Airforce Service Pilots (WASPs). Women in each of these branches worked in a variety of jobs ranging from administrative roles to service and labor. None of the positions allowed women into combat, but many placed them in or near battlefields where their lives were in danger.

As director of the WAAC, Hobby, *right*, was an effective recruiter.

The WAAC, SPARS, WAVES, and WASPs all used women in a variety of positions during the war. More than 1,000 women served in the WASPs program, which was the first to allow women to fly military aircraft.[6] These pilots transported military cargo and flew planes from factories to military bases. Although they did not fly in combat, they did free up thousands of male pilots.

There were many new opportunities for women during World War II, but there were many problems for them as well. American servicewomen did not receive the same pay, ranks, or benefits as men. Members of the WAAC, for example, faced many restrictions and limited physical training because they were not expected to see combat. They were denied overseas pay despite being sent overseas. More than 500 American servicewomen died in World War II.[7] Sixteen died from enemy fire. The others died from causes such as sickness, automobile accidents, and plane crashes.[8]

OVETA CULP HOBBY

Oveta Culp Hobby was born on January 19, 1905, in Killeen, Texas. She married *Houston Post* publisher William P. Hobby and took a research editor position at the paper. After establishing the WAC, Hobby built it to 100,000 members by April 1944.[11] She resigned as head of the WAC in July 1945 and received the Distinguished Service Medal for her leadership. In 1953, President Dwight D. Eisenhower appointed her as the first Secretary of the Department of Health, Education, and Welfare. She was the only woman in Eisenhower's cabinet. Hobby returned to the *Houston Post* in 1955 and became its publisher when her husband died in 1964. In 1996, she was inducted into the National Women's Hall of Fame. Hobby died on August 16, 1995.

Women Nurses

Women also served as military and civilian nurses during World War II. At the beginning of the war, the army listed fewer than 1,000 nurses in its service. By the end of the war, that number had grown to 59,000.[9] The navy also saw a surge of nurses during the war. Prior to Pearl Harbor, there were approximately 800 active duty naval nurses. By the end of the war, there were 10,000.[10]

Some American military nurses were kept on the home front, where they cared for wounded or ill soldiers. Others were sent overseas, where their duties ranged drastically. Some nurses were assigned

Reba Whittle

World War II flight nurses faced enemy gunfire while transporting wounded soldiers.

Reba Whittle was born in Texas in 1919. Soon after attending nursing school, she joined the US Army Air Forces as a nurse. She trained as a flight nurse and was soon stationed in the United Kingdom. Her duties there were to assist in transporting wounded soldiers from continental Europe back to the United Kingdom.

On September 27, 1944, Whittle was flying from the United Kingdom to France when German troops shot down her plane. She and the flight's crew were wounded and forced to march to a German prison camp. Whittle was held at the camp for five months. While she was there, the Germans allowed her to care for sick and wounded prisoners of war (POWs). After her release, Whittle was awarded the Purple Heart and the Air Medal for her service.

Whittle was the only female POW during World War II. The US government did not reveal this fact until 1992. Many people believe the government feared the public would react negatively to the news of a woman held in a prison camp.

to the front lines. They wore helmets, carried backpacks full of supplies, and rushed through the battlefield to help the wounded. Often, the only distinguishing part of their uniform was the white band with a red cross they wore on their upper arm. Enemies could easily kill them. Nurses often dragged wounded soldiers out of the line of fire, constructed makeshift hospitals, and supervised patient care while in the field.

Nurses also played a crucial role in evacuating injured and ill soldiers from the front lines. They helped set up temporary field hospitals, where they treated and attempted to stabilize wounded soldiers until they could either return to battle or be transported to a larger hospital farther from the front lines. Field hospitals were hastily constructed and lacked important medical supplies, but nurses were very successful. Nearly 85 percent of the soldiers who were operated on in field hospitals survived.[12]

Nurses also helped transport soldiers from field hospitals to permanent hospitals. They

AFRICAN-AMERICAN WOMEN IN WORLD WAR II

When World War II began, the US Army was still segregated. It didn't integrate until after the war in 1948. Only a small number of African-American nurses were permitted to enlist due to an official quota. In 1943, for example, only 160 black nurses were allowed to enlist.[13] This group was assigned to care for black troops. However, in 1944, the quota was eliminated and more black nurses were allowed to join. By the end of the war, black nurses had served essential roles in the South Pacific, Africa, the United Kingdom, and Burma. African-American women also served in the WAC. Notably, the 6888th Central Postal Directory Battalion was stationed in London, United Kingdom. Major Charity Edna Adams led the battalion, nicknamed "Six Triple Eight." Many considered a decline in morale to be the result of troops not receiving mail from home. The army sent Six Triple Eight to London to help with the situation. These women sorted through a frigid, dark warehouse filled with a backlog of packages and mail meant for soldiers.

World War II field hospital nurses in France

accompanied soldiers in ambulances, trucks, and planes. These trips were often very dangerous and involved traveling near battlegrounds. Medical trucks, ambulances, and designated medical evacuation planes were marked with a large red cross on a white background to tell enemies not to attack. However, many evacuation planes also carried military cargo and were not marked with the cross for protection. These flights were often in danger of being shot down by enemies.

Wartime Bravery

The brave women who served during World War II volunteered for many reasons. Some served out of pride and nationalism. Others were compelled to protect their country in whatever way possible. Some wanted to show their children a good example of patriotism. And others wanted to find glory in war.

Regardless of their motives, the women who participated in the war effort were all faced with cultural barriers. People were simply not used to seeing women perform the duties traditionally taken on by men. Women during World War II continually proved they were able and willing to take on new, difficult, and often dangerous tasks. These skills were invaluable and would serve them in the next war.

TOKYO ROSE

American-born Iva Toguri was a Japanese radio personality whose anti-American propaganda under the persona "Tokyo Rose" became famous. Tokyo Rose's radio program was designed to entertain US troops and to discourage them from fighting against Japan. She used her seductive voice and flawless English to tell US soldiers that they were acting like "boneheads" and that their girlfriends back home were cheating on them. After the war, Toguri was returned to the United States, where she was convicted of treason. She was imprisoned for six years.

WACs tour Fisherman's Wharf in San Francisco, California, in 1951.

CHAPTER FOUR

Women Game Changers

When millions of men left their jobs to fight in World War II, the US government asked women to step in and fill jobs they left behind. When the war ended, men returned to their old jobs. Women were asked to once again do their part to help their country. Many quit their jobs and returned to their roles as wives and mothers.

Many women were deeply unhappy about leaving their jobs. Some women were even fired to make room for male veterans. The jobs that remained for women were often called "pink collar." They were typically secretarial or clerical positions. They paid poorly and many women found them unchallenging and unsatisfying. Roles as homemakers, mothers, and wives were considered more suitable for women.

Women Remain in the Military

One of the few areas in which women could still hope to find work was the US military. Army and navy nurses remained in high demand, as wounded soldiers needed continued care after the war. Women serving in the WAC were able to continue their work. In 1948, the US Congress even passed a bill that made the WAC a permanent branch of the US Army. Many women in the WAVES program were able to remain in uniform long after the war had ended.

However, even in the military, roles for women were changing. Many women who had enjoyed high-level jobs found themselves demoted or taking on secretarial work. The WASP program was disbanded. Many women simply decided to leave the armed services because they felt unwelcome.

Women in the Cold War

The United States fought alongside the Soviet Union in World War II. But it was a tense alliance that became even more strained in the years after the war. The Soviets resented the United States for waiting until 1944 to invade Europe. Without the delay, they believed, millions of Russian deaths could have been prevented. The Soviets also begrudged the United States for severing diplomatic relations following the Russian Revolution of 1917. This political separation continued for 16 years and had long-lasting effects.

Tensions between the United States and the Soviet Union were so high, both nations prepared for a conflict. Each side stockpiled nuclear weapons with the capacity to kill millions of people. The world nervously watched both superpowers. Americans built bomb shelters in their backyards and

An American housewife poses with supplies for a bomb shelter.

children practiced bomb drills in school. The US government began investigating and arresting Americans who supported communist ideas.

This time became known as the Cold War. The conflict was mainly between the United States and the Soviet Union, but other nations were involved. Cuba, Germany, Mexico, Egypt, Japan, Panama, Czechoslovakia, Korea, and Vietnam were all Cold War participants. The conflict lasted from 1947 until 1991.[1] Nations grew deeply suspicious of one another and spying became a widespread activity. Organizations such as the Central Intelligence Agency (CIA) played an important role in the Cold War. It recruited, trained, and employed spies. It also hunted down spies from other countries.

Women played an integral role in the Cold War. They took on essential jobs in the CIA, the National Security Agency (NSA), and the NSA's Signals Intelligence division (SIGINT). They worked as administrators, technicians, and scientists.

Outside of governmental agencies, women worked as journalists documenting the tense events.

WOMEN IN THE KGB

The KGB was the Soviet Union's secret intelligence agency. At the peak of the Cold War, it employed approximately 500,000 people. Many of these employees were women.[2] An unknown number of female KGB spies lived in the United States during the Cold War. They were often beautiful, intelligent, and socially outgoing. They took advantage of the idea that American women should be homemakers rather than career women. They posed as housewives, living with unmarried male KGB spies, and gathered valuable information from unsuspecting American men.

Following World War II, many countries used complex encoding systems for their secret communications to prevent other countries from understanding their secret messages. In the United States, agents at the NSA worked hard to decrypt these coded messages. They used a decryption project codenamed VENONA to do this. A female NSA employee named Gene Grabeel created VENONA in 1943. It used mathematical formulas and careful analysis to break down coded messages. Many women played essential roles in making VENONA a success. Linguist Marie Meyer used her knowledge of the Russian language to help crack the codes and taught Russian language classes to other NSA agents.

FEMALE SPY HEROES

Some stories of female espionage seem to come right out of an exciting spy novel. Elizabeth Swantek was an American spy during the Cold War. Trained in survival techniques, parachuting, and wireless communication, she worked with the CIA to hire and train spies to infiltrate the Soviet Union and send back information. In the course of her career with the CIA, she posed as a journalist, a tour director, a secretary, and even a girlfriend. On one mission, she used a hidden camera in her bra to take photos of potential targets.

Women also took on covert roles during the Cold War. Under false identities, they infiltrated high levels of foreign governments, posing as secretaries, clerks, or wives or girlfriends of important officials. These brave spies risked their lives to deliver valuable information back to the US government.

In the 1950s and 1960s, American culture pushed women out of the workforce and back into the home. Although many women accepted

Linguist Meredith Gardner works on the VENONA project.

this change, some fought to remain active in the military and civilian workforce. These women achieved extraordinary accomplishments and helped to keep Americans safe from nuclear war.

COMPUTERS FOR SPYING

Although espionage might seem like a glamorous and fast-paced business, it often involves a lot of slow, detailed work. During the Cold War, agents at the NSA were tasked with sifting through enormous amounts of information as they searched for clues about Soviet activity. One woman made this job easier. Dorothy Blum was a technical expert working for the NSA. She drastically changed the way agents looked through coded data. Blum created computer programs capable of sorting, processing, and manipulating data automatically. This made the work of NSA agents much easier.

Women marines watch a special
weapons demonstration.

CHAPTER FIVE

Women in the Korean War

O n June 25, 1950, soldiers from Soviet-supported North Korea invaded US-supported South Korea. There was one US Army nurse on duty in South Korea: Captain Viola B. McConnell. Immediately after the hostilities began, McConnell worked frantically to evacuate more than 600 American people from Korea.[1] This group included sick children, pregnant women, and many weak elderly people. McConnell used ingenuity and finesse to turn a 12-passenger Norwegian freight boat into a refugee ferry. She even managed to set up a place to care for the sick onboard the ship. After delivering the refugees safely to Japan, McConnell requested to be assigned in South Korea again. Her request was granted, and she returned to South Korea to continue caring for soldiers. She was later given the Bronze Star and the Oak Leaf Cluster military awards for her outstanding performance.

The Korean War

Though the Korean War (1950–1953) was fought thousands of miles from American soil, it held enormous importance for the United States. The conflict between North and South Korea involved the spread of communism. The United States was adamantly opposed to communist nations. Within a month, the United States entered the war in support of South Korea. This was the first military conflict of the Cold War.

People around the world worried the war would escalate and eventually involve the Soviet Union and China. If this happened, many feared another world war could erupt.

The servicemen and servicewomen who had remained in the military following World War II, along with reserves, were immediately recalled to active duty. But there were not enough active-duty personnel. The United States armed forces needed members very quickly. At the outset of the Korean War, there were only 22,000 women serving in the US military. By the end of the war, that number grew to more than 120,000.[2] Women served in a variety of roles in the WAC, Women in the Air Force (WAF), WAVES, and Women Marines.

Nurses Serve

As in previous conflicts, many American women served as military nurses. However, at the outset of the war, they were incredibly rare. Two months after the war broke out, there were only 100 army nurses in South Korea.

SEXISM IN THE MILITARY

Females serving in the military during the Korean War were often subjected to overt sexism. The jobs they were assigned were considered appropriate for a woman's temperament and intellect. In other words, they were easy and not too stressful. Part of their job training often involved etiquette and cosmetics lessons. Many women found this extremely insulting. A large number of women who served in the Korean War had also served during World War II, and they completed their often dangerous and stressful jobs admirably.

US military officials scrambled to recruit and train new nurses to handle the overwhelming medical needs of combat soldiers. Finally, in July 1951, there were 3,200 army nurses serving in Korea, though this number was still too small.[3]

One element of the Korean War was Mobile Army Surgical Hospital (MASH) units, which were temporary medical tents set up near battlegrounds. Army nurses and physicians staffed these tents to handle injuries and illnesses soldiers sustained in combat. Because MASH units were designed to follow soldiers as they fought, they were often located within range of enemy fire. Eunice Coleman, a MASH nurse, remembered one incident when her mobile hospital was attacked. She and the other nurses in her unit retreated to a ditch. Coleman said:

> The whole sky was lit up by gunfire and burning vehicles. . . . About sun up we got out of the ditch and started treating the wounded. All that day we worked on the roadside operating and treating for shock. We lost eight men and a number of supply vehicles.[4]

Nurse Mary Daly cares for a wounded soldier in a MASH unit in Korea.

Nurses didn't care for only wounded soldiers on the ground. Many soldiers needed sophisticated medical help unavailable in MASH units. Army, navy, and air force nurses transported wounded and ill soldiers on trucks, boats, and planes to hospitals. These evacuation missions were often extremely dangerous and involved crossing through air, water, and land that was under attack. In the course of the war, air force nurses alone helped to evacuate more than 350,000 American soldiers out of Korea.[5] Seventeen servicewomen died during the Korean War. They were all nurses.

African-American Nurses

After World War II, many African-American WACs, such as Harriet West Waddy, went on to play major roles in the American civil rights movement. In 1948, President

Harry S. Truman signed an executive order stating the US military must treat people equally, regardless of their "race, color, religion, or national origin."[6] Before this order, only very small numbers of African-American women were permitted to enlist in the US Army, Navy, Marine Corps, and Air Force. Only 2 percent of the people in each branch could be African Americans.[7]

During the Korean War, many African-American nurses served in Korea, Japan, and Hawaii. African Americans in the WAC also served on bases in Japan and the Philippines. Despite performing well, these women faced discrimination and reported being overlooked for promotions.

Noncombat Roles for Women

Women worked in noncombat roles to free up military men to join the fight. They worked in administration, transportation, postal services, and also served in high ranks of leadership. One leader was Staff Sergeant Hazel Lindahl. In 1952, Lindahl was camp sergeant major of more than 40,000 marines at Camp Lejeune in Jacksonville, North Carolina.[8] Sergeant majors are senior officers

ANNA MAE HAYS AND AN AMAZING FIELD HOSPITAL

Even though MASH units were temporary structures, they were able to care for huge numbers of patients safely and efficiently. In 1950, Army Nurse Anna Mae Hays mobilized with the Fourth Field Hospital and was part of a military landing in Inchon, South Korea. Her hospital cared for more than 25,000 patients in only 10 months. In one night, she and the other medical staff treated more than 700 wounded soldiers.[9] Hays worked through frigid winter temperatures with insufficient supplies and overwhelming numbers of wounded patients. However, she remained calm and did her work heroically. Hays remained in the army and in 1970 became the first woman in military history to attain the rank of general.

WACs Harriet West Waddy, *left*, and Irma Cayton, *right*, work on recruiting reports.

who have many leadership responsibilities, including acting as spokespeople for their troops.

While women took on more military responsibility, obstacles remained toward equality. The roles offered to women during the Korean War were more limited than those offered during World War II. Social ideals about femininity and a woman's role at home dominated even the military world. A recruiting pamphlet from 1951 cautioned,

> In authorizing job assignments for women, particular care is taken to see that the job does not involve a type of duty that violates our concept of proper employment for sisters and girlfriends. In the military transport field, for example, women do not drive heavy trucks.[10]

The Korean War ended in 1953. Approximately 5 million people, both

An army nurse assists a helicopter crew member with a wounded soldier at Brooke Army Medical Center in San Antonio, Texas.

civilians and soldiers, lost their lives in this major conflict.[11] The women who served in Korea did so bravely and heroically. But for them, the battle for military equality was far from over.

Photographer Dickey Chapelle
took this image of South
Vietnamese soldiers exiting a
US Army helicopter during the
Vietnam War.

CHAPTER SIX

Women in the Vietnam War

I n November 1965, photographer Dickey Chapelle was accompanying a group of US soldiers in Vietnam. Born Georgette Louise Meyer, Chapelle was no stranger to dangerous battlegrounds. She had talked her way into photographing soldiers in the trenches on Iwo Jima during World War II and had snapped photos of battle during the Korean War. Her photographs were published in newspapers and magazines around the world, and she was a well-respected war journalist.

During this mission, however, tragedy struck. A marine accidentally stepped on a booby trap in front of Chapelle, it exploded and sent shrapnel flying. The famous photographer was hit in the neck. Chapelle died along with four marines.[1]

The Vietnam War

The Vietnam War began in 1954. The conflict involved South Vietnam and communist North Vietnam, along with the Viet Cong, the North's allies living in the south. As with the Korean War, the United States entered the conflict because it opposed North Vietnam's communist ideals. The war was very unpopular among Americans, who believed the United States should stay out of the foreign conflict. By 1968, a political poll showed 50 percent of the country disapproved of the way President Lyndon B. Johnson was handling the war. Many people started openly rejecting the United States' participation in the war. In 1973, the United States withdrew its forces from Vietnam, partly due to the social pressure. The war ended two years later, and North and South Vietnam became a unified communist country. Many Americans believed their nation's participation in the war was senseless, pointless, and ineffective.

American troops suffered heavy losses during the Vietnam War. More than one in ten US soldiers were injured or killed during the conflict. It was even more brutal for the Vietnamese.

AFRICAN-AMERICAN WOMEN IN VIETNAM

Race was an important issue during the Vietnam War. African Americans in the United States were struggling for equality, respect, and even safety at home, yet they were drafted into military service alongside white American men. Many black Americans deeply resented this. African-American women who served faced both racism and the sexism plaguing their white peers. When asked about her experiences as a black nurse in Vietnam, Clotilde Bowen said,

> Many assume you are weak and inferior, not very capable. . . but it's not so much because you are black, but because you are a woman. The Army is learning, often painfully, how to accept blacks as people. But it is still uptight about women.[2]

US Army nurses Gladys E. Sepulveda, *left*,
and Lois Ferrari rest at Cam Ranh Bay in
South Vietnam.

Including the 58,000 American soldiers who died during the war, more than 3 million people were killed.[3] Vietnamese civilians accounted for more than one-half of this number.

Women Serve

Very little is recorded about the role women played in the Vietnam War. However, they were undoubtedly an important part of the conflict. Approximately 11,000 US military women were stationed in Vietnam during the war. Nearly 90 percent of those women were army, navy, and air force nurses.[4] They cared for the heavy casualty load of the war, and they worked to train the South Vietnamese in nursing skills so they could care for their own wounded.

Women also held important WAC positions. These were noncombat jobs, such as air traffic controllers, intelligence officers, physicians, and clerks. WAC troops were stationed in Saigon, which is now Ho Chi Minh City, and other important military hubs throughout the country. Though they were a small group, numbering approximately 150 women at its peak, the members of WAC were essential to the war effort.[5]

WOMEN ON HOSPITAL SHIPS

Many navy nurses were stationed onboard military hospital ships, such as the USS *Repose*. Often called "The Angel of the Orient," the *Repose* was staffed by 29 US military nurses. When fighting was intense, as many as 200 wounded soldiers were brought onboard the ship by helicopter in only 24 hours. These courageous nurses worked seamlessly with other members of the crew to care for the wounded. Nurse Frances Shea Buckley remembered, "A bonding developed among all crew members, unlike any I had ever experienced before or since Vietnam. Crew members, whether ship's company or hospital personnel, truly cared about the patients."[6]

Women also served in the air force during the Vietnam War, in a group called the Women in the Air Force (WAF). These women took on roles normally occupied by male air force personnel. They worked in aircraft maintenance, intelligence, public affairs, and other departments.

The Vietnam War was largely fought using guerilla tactics. This meant there were few official front lines. Rather, there were pockets of small but organized groups of the opposition who were constantly ambushing American troops. Women who were serving in noncombat roles were still very much in danger of enemy fire.

Women continued to face obstacles and discrimination in the military during the Vietnam War. Despite the claims in recruiting brochures that the military offered "challenging jobs with unlimited opportunities" for women, most challenging and technical positions were open only to men.[7] In fact, the Vietnam War continued to reverse the progress women achieved during World War II. WAC training involving weapons drills and camping skills was replaced with lessons on lipstick, nail polish, and fashion. Servicewomen were often expected to dress in skirts and heels, even in dangerous combat zones. And they were often denied promotions based on their gender alone. In 1967, Congress finally voted to allow women to achieve higher ranks, such as general and admiral. But few women experienced immediate benefits from this change in policy.

Nonmilitary Roles for Women

The military was not the only place for women to serve in the Vietnam War. Women were also present in the conflict as war journalists. More than 300 female writers, photographers, and war

First Lieutenant Sharon Ann Lane

When First Lieutenant Sharon Ann Lane was first stationed in Vietnam, she was assigned to the Intensive Care Unit (ICU) for American soldiers at the 312th Evacuation Hospital in Chu Lai. However, days after she arrived, she was reassigned to a ward made up entirely of injured and ill Vietnamese. Her patients were very sick and she worked 12-hour days, five days a week. She spent her free time caring for injured American soldiers housed in the hospital's ICU.

On June 8, 1969, the Viet Cong fired rockets into Lane's hospital. She was immediately killed. Lane was the only nurse in Vietnam to be killed by enemy fire. She was later awarded the Purple Heart and the Bronze Star with "V" Device, which designates "participation in acts of heroism involving conflict with an armed enemy."[8] Lane also received the National Defense Service Medal, the Vietnam Service Medal, the National Order of Vietnam Medal, and the Vietnamese Gallantry Cross with Palm.

(1943–1969)

correspondents went to Vietnam to document the war. Although
many of these women captured amazing stories and achieved
never-before-seen access to war,
they were not all welcomed by the
troops or their male colleagues.
A US marine once shouted at
reporter Gloria Emerson, "What
the hell did they send a woman
here for? War is a man's business!"[9]

Women were also present in
Vietnam as civilian volunteers.
Organizations such as the Red

FEMALE CASUALTIES

Thousands of American women served in Vietnam, both as members of the military and as volunteers with civilian organizations. Approximately 11,000 women served there in the US military, and thousands more worked with organizations such as the Red Cross.[10] In total, 67 American women lost their lives in the Vietnam War. Eight were members of the US military. Seven were US Army nurses and one was a US Air Force nurse. Fifty-nine female civilians were killed during the war. They were journalists, volunteers, missionaries, and other nonmilitary workers.[11]

Cross, Peace Corps, and Catholic Relief services deployed thousands of women to Vietnam to help in the war effort. These women provided food, medical care, and other assistance to the troops.

The Vietnam War was a controversial conflict. Many Americans did not support it. This made it complicated for women who wanted to serve in the US armed forces. Some chose to abstain from the fight because they did not believe the United States should be involved. Others chose to take the opportunity to gain access to jobs within the US military, even though they could be very dangerous.

The women who served during Vietnam helped establish roles for women in future conflicts. They also helped keep American troops as safe, healthy, and well supplied as possible.

Women in *Military Schools*

In 1975, President Gerald Ford signed a bill requiring US military academies to start admitting women the following school year. More than 300 women rushed to enroll at the US Naval Academy, the US Coast Guard Academy, the US Air Force Academy, and the US Military Academy, otherwise known as West Point.

The first female class at West Point had 119 eager, smart, and strong women. In the course of four years, they were pushed mentally and physically to meet the academy's rigid standards for all students, both male and female. One female cadet recalled:

> *Many women suffered injuries from the road marches with full gear and running in combat boots or our suede Converse sneakers up and down hills for miles at a time at a pace often under 8-minutes per mile. . . . I decided early on that I would pass out before I let myself drop out of a run.*[12]

In 1980, 62 proud female cadets made history by graduating from West Point. Some state military schools waited much longer to allow women to enroll. The first female student was allowed into the Citadel, the South Carolina Military College, in 1993. The Virginia Military Institute did not allow female students until the Supreme Court forced it to in 1996. Valley Forge, otherwise known as the Military Academy of Pennsylvania, was the last holdout. It did not admit women until 2006.

One of the 62 female cadets who
graduated from West Point in 1980

A female marine arrives at
a Saudi Arabian air base in
August 1990.

CHAPTER SEVEN

Women in the Gulf War

The Persian Gulf War (1990–1991) began when Saddam Hussein, the leader of Iraq, invaded neighboring Kuwait in 1990. Other nations, such as Egypt, Saudi Arabia, and the United States, objected to the invasion. The United Nations Security Council demanded Iraq withdraw from Kuwait. When Iraq ignored this order, the United States began preparing for a war. In a mission known as Operation Desert Shield, it began stockpiling planes and ships in Saudi Arabia. In January 1991, the United States launched a huge air attack called Operation Desert Storm. The air assault was very effective. Most Iraqi troops either fled Kuwait or surrendered.

The Persian Gulf War lasted only eight months. The United States' participation in the conflict was even shorter: it was involved for only 42 days. However, the effect this war had on the role of women in the military was lasting.

Changes for Women

Leading up to the Persian Gulf War, women achieved many new ranks and rights within the US military. In 1978, the WAC disbanded and women were fully integrated in the US Army. The draft was also repealed after the Vietnam War in 1973. The US armed forces were now all-volunteer. At that time, the number of active-duty women in the four branches of the armed forces was 45,000. By 1980, the number rose to 171,000 active female members. In addition to admittance into the most prestigious military academies, women attained new assignments previously barred to their gender. In 1974, an army woman became the first female military helicopter pilot. In 1983, the first navy woman completed the rigorous Test Pilot School. In 1985, the top graduate from the Coast Guard Academy was a woman.[1] In 1991, Darlene Iskra became the first female to be appointed commanding officer of a US Navy ship.

Servicewomen were making strides by conquering new roles, ranks, and occupations. They were breaking down barriers and proving they were capable of working in many military fields.

SHIP LEADER

In 1991, Darlene Iskra became the first woman to command a ship in the US Navy. The USS *Opportune* is a 213-foot- (65 m) long, 2,000-ton (1,800 metric ton) warship. Iskra remembered her first days as the ship's captain, "I was scared to death . . . but once we got out to sea, I felt pretty good."[2] The navy members on board Iskra's ship were not affected by her gender. The ship's second in command, Lieutenant Dave Randall, said, "As far as the crew and I are concerned, Commander Iskra's first name is 'Captain.' There is no difference."[3]

Iskra was appointed commanding officer of the
USS *Opportune*.

Women Deploy

The Persian Gulf War saw an enormous deployment of female military personnel. There were
40,000 women who served in the US Army, Navy, Air Force, and Marine Corps.[4] They made up
11 percent of all active-duty service people. And unlike in previous wars, the majority of servicewomen
were not nurses. In fact, less than one-half of the women in this war worked in medical specialties or
administration. Instead, they were working beside male comrades, driving trucks, flying helicopters,
and directing artillery. Women were not kept from the front lines of battle. In fact, 71 percent of
women in the Gulf War reported having at least one exposure to combat.[5]

New weapons, aircraft, and communications technology made the Gulf War an unprecedented battlefield for both men and women. Attack jets with GPS and stealth technology allowed pilots to hit precise targets while avoiding enemy fire. Satellite imaging and communications helped advisers know exactly what was happening on the battlefield, even from thousands of miles away. It also helped the media stay updated on the conflict in real time. Viewers at home saw much of what the troops were up to, from their combat missions to their downtime. This was a change in war journalism that had a strong effect on the role of women in the armed forces.

Women in the Line of Fire

One element of the war the media highlighted was the fact that, although women were not allowed in combat roles, they were very much in danger. US Representative Patricia Schroeder said,

The Persian Gulf helped collapse the whole chivalrous notion that women could be kept out of danger in a war. We saw that the theater of operations had no strict combat zone, that Scud missiles were not gender-specific—they could hit both sexes and, unfortunately, did.[6]

Americans responded to this in different ways. Some believed women had equal rights and, therefore, should be allowed to fight in the same way men did. Others believed war was too dangerous for women, and their presence in combat areas could compromise the success of their male comrades.

In the 1990s, military leaders were under intense social and political pressure to embrace the influx of females in the armed services. It was considered taboo for them to discourage women from taking on certain jobs, even though they were still not allowed into combat. Although this social pressure was beneficial for female soldiers—it allowed them into jobs previously unavailable to women—some people saw it as harmful. Male colleagues were discouraged from bringing up concerns about women in the military. They were

PREGNANCIES AT SEA

During the Gulf War, 10 percent of the female service members on board the USS *Acadia* became pregnant after seven months of duty in the Gulf War.[7] Many news media outlets saw this statistic as evidence that women should not be involved in the war. They called the naval vessel a "Love Boat" and made jokes about improper behavior occurring while at war. However, naval officials claimed no service members on board the ship acted improperly. The navy has strict rules stating sexual relationships between men and women are strictly forbidden while on duty. They clarified that some of the women were pregnant before they boarded the ship, and others became pregnant while the ship was docked at ports.

overwhelmingly told to accept and embrace women soldiers and not to ask questions. The motives behind this acceptance were good, but caused problems for women in the military.

Making Accommodations for Females

Although women in the military did not want special treatment, such as safer deployments, they did need some changes to traditional accommodation. Separate showers, medical care, and sleeping quarters were all deemed necessary for servicewomen. Some people feared these accommodations would disrupt the sense of brotherhood in the US armed forces. Others believed it was necessary to make sure servicewomen were well cared for. Not all servicewomen agreed with these accommodations. Some wanted to sleep in the same bunks as the rest of the troops. Others believed being singled out for any reason created distance between male and female soldiers.

One of the greatest challenges women in the military experienced during the Gulf War did not come from enemy fire. Rather, it was the threat and often reality of sexual harassment, discrimination, and assault from their male comrades. At least 24 army servicewomen were raped during the Gulf War. These assaults occurred in many different environments, such as while on guard duty or while showering. Men who ranked higher than their victims committed almost all of the rapes. In many cases, the victims waited weeks or even months to report their assaults. They said they worried they would not be believed or even feared they would be punished for speaking out.

Many accused the military of keeping the high incidence of sexual harassment and assaults secret from the media. Army officials dismissed this notion, saying the number of sexual assaults that occurred within the army were consistent with those in a similar civilian population. "If you took a city of 300,000, like Pittsburgh," one official said, "how many cases of sexual assault or rape would you have in a year's period?"[8] His question indicated he believed the violence perpetrated against female service members was no greater within the army than outside it. However, many critics have noted no amount of sexual violence is acceptable, and female service members should feel protected within their ranks.

The Gulf War's Effect

In some ways, the Gulf War was an enormous success for women in the US military. They were able to serve alongside men in a wide variety of military jobs on the front lines of a global conflict. However, in other ways, the war highlighted the issues that continued to hold women back. Despite the fact that they still were not allowed into official combat roles, and they were still fighting against the idea that women were not fit for war, 16 American servicewomen died during Desert Storm.[9]

SEXUAL ASSAULT FROM THE ENEMY

In 1991, flight surgeon Rhonda Cornum's helicopter crashed. She suffered from extensive wounds, including two broken arms, an injured knee, and a bullet wound in her shoulder. Iraqi soldiers captured Cornum and her surviving crew and took them prisoner. While in captivity, Cornum was sexually molested by her Iraqi guard. Although many in the media pointed to Cornum's experience as evidence that women should not be at war, Cornum disagreed:

> Every 15 seconds in America, some woman is assaulted. Why are they worried about a woman getting assaulted once every 10 years in a war overseas? It's ridiculous. Clearly it's an emotional argument they use . . . because they can't think of a rational one.[10]

Despite new opportunities during the Gulf War, female soldiers still struggled.

The media both helped and hurt their cause. Some news anchors profiled amazing female warriors flying helicopters, fueling fighter jets, and sailing warships. They showed American viewers how strong female soldiers could be. But other media outlets focused on the idea that women were weak, easily injured, and unfit for battle. The struggle for female soldiers was far from over.

DON'T ASK DON'T TELL

During World War II, the US government banned homosexuals from serving in the military. President Bill Clinton lifted this ban in 1993 with the Don't Ask, Don't Tell policy. Military personnel were told "don't ask, don't tell, don't pursue, and don't harass" other service people about their sexuality.[11] Although this permitted gays and lesbians to serve in the military, it forbade them from being open about their sexuality. Many people believed this was discrimination. They also believed the policy failed to protect gay and lesbian service people from being discharged for their sexuality. In 2011, Don't Ask, Don't Tell was officially repealed. Gays and lesbians were finally allowed to serve openly in the US military.

US Marine Jodi Maroney prepares to perform a communications check on a helicopter at a Gulf region air base in 2003.

CHAPTER EIGHT

Women in Afghanistan and Iraq

O n September 11, 2001, Heather "Lucky" Penney had just finished a training flight at Andrews Air Force Base in Camp Springs, Maryland. She was sitting at a briefing table when she learned a plane had flown into one of the World Trade Center towers in New York City, New York. Penney and a group of pilots were shocked when another plane hit the other tower, followed by a third plane crashing into the Pentagon. After learning a fourth plane was hijacked in the air, Penney and her team went into action. Penney and Colonel Marc Sasseville sprinted to their unarmed jets and rocketed into the air. Their target was United Airlines Flight 93. "We wouldn't be shooting it down. We'd be ramming the aircraft. . . . I would essentially be a kamikaze pilot," Penney said.[1] Sasseville would aim for the cockpit, while Penney would aim for the tail.

Ultimately, Penney and Sasseville did not have to bring down the flight. The passengers onboard bravely brought it down themselves before the terrorist hijackers were able to crash the plane into the White House. Later that day, Penney helped clear the airspace around Washington, DC, and safely escorted President George W. Bush onboard Air Force One.

Penney was only one of the female heroes of September 11, 2001. She and other women rushed to defend the United States in the moments and days following the attacks. Though women were still officially banned from combat, they responded to the attack on US soil by enlisting in the military in a variety of noncombat positions.

The Wars in Afghanistan and Iraq

The hijackers who had brought down the planes on September 11 were part of a terrorist group known as al-Qaeda. The Taliban, the ultraconservative political and religious group in control of Afghanistan, provided al-Qaeda sanctuary. The United States responded to the terrorist attacks by declaring war on Afghanistan in 2001. Two years later, the United States declared war on Iraq following suspicions the country supported al-Qaeda and possessed weapons of mass destruction (WMDs). This accusation was later proved false—Iraq was not in possession of any WMDs.

A female Marine plays with an Iraqi child in 2007.

The wars in Afghanistan and Iraq were complex and involved many different political players and motivations. But they overlapped in the American consciousness as wars against terrorism. Women were heavily involved in these wars as peacekeepers, aggressors, terrorists, and soldiers.

From 1994 until 2013, a US military ban prevented women from participating in ground combat. This did not, of course, keep women from dangerous situations in which they were faced with enemy fire. The ban played more of a political role, assuring people who did not want women in combat that these soldiers were not allowed to participate.

Women Fight

In 2003, the marines launched a special all-female unit that played a crucial role in Middle Eastern war zones. Soldiers were often required to interview and search local citizens near combat zones, but it was culturally inappropriate for these interactions to occur between male soldiers and female civilians. Therefore, the Lioness Program was created to allow female soldiers to conduct these interviews and searches. The program was hugely successful. Female soldiers were able to establish friendly rapport with local women and gain valuable intelligence, all without violating important cultural norms.

Women who served in the Iraq war were officially barred from combat for the duration of the entire war, which ended in 2011. Women in Afghanistan faced similar restrictions. However, these rules did not prevent female service members from performing dangerous, yet essential roles. Women worked as truck drivers, military police, helicopter pilots, medics, and more. The unpredictable nature of both the Iraq and Afghanistan wars meant women faced spontaneous attacks even though they were not technically participating in ground combat. Improvised explosive devices (IEDs), sniper attacks, and suicide bombs were all threats to women in noncombat roles.

In 2010, the army formed an elite, female-only unit called the Cultural Support Team (CST). This unit served alongside Army Special Operations teams and worked to gain

FEMALE ENGAGEMENT TEAMS

Following the success of the Lioness Program, the US Marine Corps established Female Engagement Teams (FETs) in Afghanistan in 2009. These were small groups of female soldiers who communicated with Afghan families. They gathered important military intelligence and also assisted with civil affairs. FETs worked to assist units of marines and special ops teams. Today, most US troops have withdrawn. Afghan men have assumed the work previously done by US FETs.

valuable intelligence from Afghan women. Just as members of the Lioness Program had done, women in the CST were able to gain essential, lifesaving information from local women while remaining respectful of Afghan customs.

Women in the CST were some of the highest-performing female troops the army had to offer. The training they endured was rigorous and intense, and for good reason. They were often sent into incredibly dangerous situations. One instructor of the CST training course told trainees:

> You are CSTs and you have a very particular job to do on the battlefield. You have to de-escalate whatever situation you are drawn into, and engage with the women and children. But we are not at war to pass out blankets and hugs. I need you to find out where the bad guys are, as quick as you can.[2]

Although these women were still not officially participating in ground combat, this distinction existed only in political terms. Their forward-deployments into hostile territories were often just as hazardous as their male peers' combat missions.

The creation of CSTs was a politically charged action. The army knew it could face pushback

ISRAELI MEN AND WOMEN IN COMBAT

Most men and women in Israel are required to serve in the country's military for a set period of approximately two years. Their required service depends on their age, occupation, and other factors. Women make up approximately one-third of the Israeli Defense Forces (IDF). They work in a wide variety of positions, from clerical jobs to special operations and ground combat. In many ways, women in the IDF are treated equally to men. This equality is reflected in the high ranks many women have achieved. Nearly one-half of Israeli lieutenants and captains are women. However, there is still room for women to grow in the IDF. The highest-ranking woman is a major general. One retired female colonel remarked on the sexism in the upper ranks of the IDF, saying that it is still very much "a boys club."[3]

Jennifer Short performs a preflight check on her aircraft at Davis-Monthan Air Force Base in Arizona.

from both enlisted service people and civilians for sending women into hostile encounters. However, army leaders also knew how useful women could be in these scenarios. Even the name Cultural Support Team reflects the delicate balance the army tried to achieve: it does not include the word *female*.

Women in Combat

In 2013, the ban on women in ground combat was lifted. The order lifting the ban pointed out, "Success in our military based solely on ability, qualifications, and performance is consistent with our values and enhances military readiness."[4] This meant the military recognized gender does not determine a soldier's ability to fight for his or her country. Former secretary of defense Leon Panetta commented on the ban being lifted, reminding people women had already been sacrificing their lives in the military for years: "They're fighting and they're dying together, and the time has come for our policies to recognize that reality."[5] Most military personnel understood this was simply a change in policy language. Women had already been occupying roles in and around combat for years. Nearly 300,000 women served in Iraq and Afghanistan, and approximately 1,000 were wounded or killed.[6] Policies keeping women from ground combat were clearly not keeping women out of danger.

The news that women would be allowed into combat was met with mixed responses. Some service members believed it was long overdue. Others thought it was a mistake. One marine, Staff Sergeant Alex Reyes, did not support the move. "It's the worst decision that the

THE FIREMAN'S CARRY

Many critics question if a small woman could carry an injured male soldier out of danger. Conservative pundit George Will wondered what would happen if "you're a 6'4" [2 m], 240-pound [109 kg] marine, and you're injured, and you need a marine next to you to carry you back to safety, and the marine next to you is a 5'4" [1.6 m] woman who weighs 115 pounds [68 kg]."[11] Will's question highlights his doubts that a woman could safely evacuate a man from danger.

Journalist Elspeth Reeve disagreed, saying, "The thing is, you don't need much upper body strength to carry a guy out of combat."[12] She points out the technique taught to all military personnel, called the fireman's carry, is actually quite easy. Female soldiers are able to use it to carry even very heavy male colleagues.[13]

military could make," he said.[7] Representative Tulsi Gabbard served with the Hawaiian National Guard in Iraq and supported the change. She said it was "great recognition . . . of all the women who are currently serving overseas, many of them in these combat type situations already."[8] Many politicians also weighed in on the issue. Republican Senator Kelly Ayotte said, "I think this is a very positive step, and it reflects the reality of what's happening, obviously, in defending our nation."[9] However, Republican Senator Tom Cotton argued women aren't physically capable of carrying out combat duties. "To have women serving in the infantry . . . could impair the mission essential task of those units, and that's been proven in study after study," Cotton said.[10]

This policy change would benefit servicewomen hoping to enter combat. Combat experience is often taken into account when service people are given promotions and can make it easier to move up in the military. Combat action badges and valor awards also help military advancement. This may make the military a more attractive lifetime career for women.

Ashley White

When she joined the Reserve Officer Training Corps (ROTC) program at Kent State University, Ashley White's peers called her "Little White." She was, after all, a petite blonde, standing only 5 feet 3 inches (1.6 m) tall. This nickname did not define her. She soon proved herself to be an outstanding athlete and corps member.

After her time in the ROTC, White went on to become a US Army Medical Service Corps Officer. In 2011, White defied the odds by becoming one of 60 women to be accepted into the army's elite CST. Soon after, her CST deployed alongside an elite special ops team in Afghanistan. On October 22, 2011, White was helping her team search the compound of a weapons maker when a bomb exploded, killing her and two others. She was the first CST member to be killed in action.

(1987–2011)

The Weight of War

Some critics of women in ground combat point to the fact that women have smaller bodies and muscles and may face greater challenges and injuries from carrying their heavy gear through a battleground. Infantry often have to carry equipment weighing 80 pounds (36 kg) or more through harsh terrain for many hours at a time.

Infantry troops carry heavy equipment into combat. From their helmets to their body armor, they can often bear loads between 60 and 100 pounds (27 and 45 kg).[14] Here is an example of what a rifle squad leader might carry into battle:

STANDARD EQUIPMENT
Weapon, such as M4 carbine with ammunition
Radio
Interceptor body armor
Two or more meals ready to eat (MREs)
Combat helmet batteries
Knee and elbow pads
Poncho
Sand/sun/dust goggles
Knife
Spare socks
Gun cleaning kit
Grenades
164 ounces (4.6 kg) of water in canteens and hydration bladder
Night vision equipment
Flashlight
Whistles

In 2013, Dr. David Cifu, national director of physical medicine and rehabilitation at the Veteran's Health Administration, voiced concerns about the risks these heavy packs pose for women's bodies. Cifu said the armed forces needs to develop better gear for female soldiers:

> *You need to go leaner and meaner. Infantry is going to go high tech and it will cost money, but it's not just a woman-thing—they've got to do this for all of them.*[15]

Army reservist Chandra Banks said it's not just about the weight but the fit. Without proper-fitting gear, she said, "it's going to make you more vulnerable and less effective."[16]

In December 2015, the US Army announced it was redeveloping both the male and female versions of combat gear. The new combat gear would be lighter and fit 94 percent of male and female soldiers.[17]

Body armor, a helmet, and essential supplies create a lot of weight for both female and male soldiers.

In the last century, many opportunities have opened up for women in the military.

CHAPTER NINE

Women in Future Wars

Women have always played crucial roles in warfare, whether by providing essential civilian support or by fighting alongside men on the front lines. As time passes, women will continue assisting in war efforts in many ways. In the US armed forces, women are holding more and more positions. They occupy approximately 15 percent of the total number of active-duty military personnel. In 2015, there were 201,400 active-duty women in the military. Of that number, 68,000 were in the US Army, 57,300 in the US Navy, 58,500 in the US Air Force, and 14,100 in the US Marine Corps.[1] They make up 16.6 percent of the commissioned officers and account for 7 percent of generals and admirals.[2]

Women are even breaking into some of the most elite, exclusive military units. In 2015, Captain Kristen Griest and First Lieutenant Shaye Haver became the first women to graduate from Army Ranger School. It is a program so grueling and demanding only 42 percent of candidates successfully

Vice Admiral Michelle Howard

(1960–)

On July 1, 2014, Michelle J. Howard made history. She became the first woman in the navy to become a four-star admiral. She was also promoted to the 38th vice-chief of naval operations. This gave her the second-highest rank in the US Navy.[3] Howard was not only the first woman to hold this prestigious rank, but also the first African American.

Howard is used to paving the way for African-American women in the military. She was part of the third class of women to graduate from the US Naval Academy in 1982. She was the first African-American woman to become a three-star officer in the military. In 1990, she became the chief engineer for the USS *Mount Hood*, and in 1992, she became the first lieutenant on the USS *Flint*. She also became the first African-American woman to command a US Navy ship when she took control of the USS *Rushmore* in 1999.

complete it.[4] Their success has highlighted that women can achieve greatness in historically male-only units. "This course has proven that every soldier, regardless of gender, can achieve his or her full potential," said US Army Secretary John McHugh.[5] In response to the successful female Rangers, the Navy SEALs program plans to accept qualified female candidates in upcoming seasons. US Army Special Forces (also known as the Green Berets) also plans to do the same.

These historic changes mean qualified women can apply for coveted spots in some of the military's most famous and specialized training programs. However, it does not mean they will be allowed to actually serve with their colleagues. Despite allowing women to attend the Army Ranger training program, the army still will not allow them to become Army Rangers. The highly trained women who have graduated as Army Rangers cannot deploy with their teammates. They can, however, use their Army Ranger status to achieve higher ranks, pay, and promotions.

Challenges for Women

In addition to struggling for acceptance in the military community, servicewomen also face other problems. Sexual harassment, discrimination, and assault are still major concerns

WOMEN IN COMBAT AROUND THE WORLD

Other than the United States, eight countries currently allow women into military combat units. These include Australia, Canada, Denmark, Egypt, France, Israel, Germany, New Zealand, and Norway.

Norway allows women in the military the unique ability to serve in any combat capacity. Norway was the first country in NATO to allow this combat freedom to women. A military researcher commented on Norway's progressive stance regarding women in combat: "The Scandinavian countries are very good at leading in gender equality, so it's no surprise that Norway should pioneer female conscription."[6]

Women continue to stand
out alongside men in all
branches of the armed forces.

within the US armed forces. In 2014, 22 percent of active-duty women experienced sexual harassment and 4 percent experienced unwanted sexual contact.[7]

Many of the struggles reported by military women echo those of working women everywhere. They often have trouble juggling family and work, citing this as a top reason for leaving the military. Some have reported believing their gender has held them back from promotions or has resulted in poor treatment from male colleagues. Military life is especially hard on heterosexual marriages when the female partner is in active duty. Divorce rates are three times higher for female soldiers than for male soldiers—9.2 percent compared with 3.3 percent.[8] These difficulties mean women in the military must often work harder than men to maintain work–life balance.

Women in the military must also confront and accept the physical differences between men and women. Statistics and medical testing have proven men are stronger in their upper bodies than women are. Military training programs used to account for the difference in male and female physiques by allowing men and women to complete different tasks to pass. For example, women would be allowed to perform a flexed-arm hang for 15 seconds instead of completing the three pull-ups required of men. However, this practice of allowing gender-unique standards may end. The military is creating new, job-specific, gender-neutral standards that every candidate must pass. These tests will account for the differences in physical ability of all candidates, not only women. Recruits hoping to work in a desk job may be required to perform a 15-second flexed-arm hang, whereas those hoping to drive tanks or engage in combat might need to perform a specific number of pull-ups. Brigadier General Brian Kelly, director of military force management policy, said, "This effort marks

Griest, *left*, and Haver, *right*, wave to their families during their graduation from Army Ranger School in 2015.

the most stringent process yet by which we are developing occupationally specific physical standards, scientifically measured against operational requirements to match mission needs."[9] Military leaders hope this gender-neutral testing approach will eliminate gender discrimination and also ensure the candidates are placed in jobs that match their strengths.

Kayla Williams, author of the 2005 book *Love My Rifle More than You: Young and Female in the US Army*, said admitting women in combat will be a great new advancement for the US military. "Let's take this step and let women keep proving what they have already proved before," Williams said.[10] Her sentiment is clear: women are ready for the challenge.

BECOMING A SEAL

Women in the US Navy will soon be able to enroll in the extremely challenging basic underwater demolition (BUD) training to become a SEAL. Before they can do so, they must complete a physical fitness test involving a timed swim, push-ups, sit-ups, pull-ups, and running.

Once enrolled in BUD training, candidates must complete many extremely difficult challenges, such as drown-proofing: an exercise that requires them to float, swim, flip, and dive underwater while both hands and feet are tied together. One of the hardest parts of BUD training is known as Hell Week. This five-and-a-half-day operational training exercise requires recruits to perform extremely difficult physical and mental tasks on less than four hours of sleep. On average, only one-fourth of SEAL candidates make it through Hell Week.

Growing
Presence

As of 2015, women accounted for 15.3 percent of active-duty personnel in the US military.

The US military is changing. It is adapting to a society with more gender equality than ever before. Since the US military became all-volunteer in 1973, the percentage of enlisted women increased from 2 percent to 14 percent in 2010.[11] The number of enlisted women grew even as the total number of all US military forces decreased by approximately 738,000 service members during the same period.[12] Statistics also show active-duty women also tend to be more racially diverse than active-duty men. In 2011, 31 percent of women were African American compared to 16 percent of men.[13]

Women continue breaking through boundaries and achieving higher and higher ranks within the armed forces. In 2015, there were 2,600 women enrolled in US military academies. Of the 71,400 deployed members of the US military, 9,200 were women. Women also had access to 90 percent of all US military occupations.[14] As women enter into new military roles, such as combat, there will surely be setbacks and controversies. But women have shown they are willing to fight.

Growth of Women in the US Military: 1973–2010

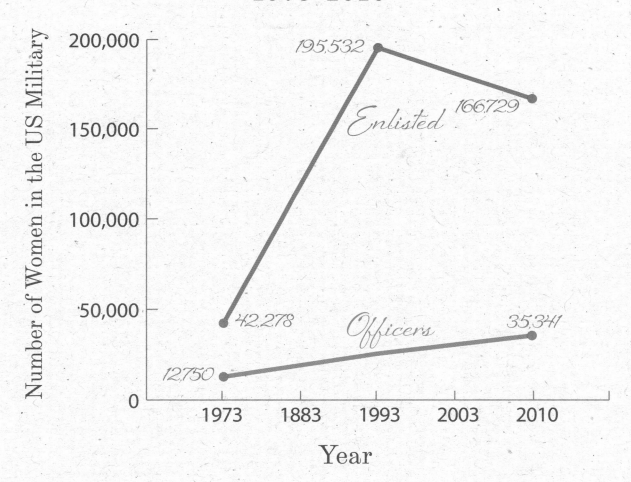

Timeline

1429

Joan of Arc leads the French army to victory over the English in Orléans, France.

1914

Franz and Sophie Ferdinand are assassinated on June 28 in Sarajevo. This event leads to the beginning of World War I.

1917

The Women's Auxiliary Army Corps (WAAC) is formed in the British armed services. This allows women to serve in noncombat roles in the armed services.

1918

The British Women's Royal Air Force is formed. This allows women to serve in noncombat roles in the Air Force.

1941

The Japanese attack Pearl Harbor on December 7, launching the United States into World War II.

1942

The WAAC is formed in the United States in May. It allows women to serve in noncombat roles in the US Army. It is later renamed the Women's Army Corps (WAC).

1943

Gene Grabeel creates the VENONA code for the National Security Agency; Elsie Ott makes her historic World War II medical evacuation flight around the world in January.

1950

Captain Viola B. McConnell successfully evacuates more than 600 Americans out of Korea at the outset of the Korean War on June 25.

1969

First Lieutenant Sharon Ann Lane is killed by enemy fire in Vietnam on June 8.

1970
Anna Mae Hays becomes the first woman in US military history to attain the rank of general.

1974
An army woman becomes the first female military helicopter pilot.

1976
Women are admitted into US military academies for the first time.

1978
The WAC disbands and women are fully integrated into the US Army.

1980
The first women graduate from West Point.

1983
The first navy woman completes the Test Pilot School.

1991
Darlene Iskra became the first woman to command a ship in the US Navy.

1994
The US military officially bars women from combat.

2013
The US military lifts the ban on women in ground combat.

2015
Kristen Griest and Shaye Haver graduate from the elite Army Rangers school.

Essential Facts

- Annie Fox serves heroically during the attacks on Pearl Harbor on December 7, 1941.

- Elsie Ott flies a groundbreaking experimental medical evacuation flight around the world in 1943.

- Gene Grabeel creates the VENONA code for the National Security Agency (NSA) in 1943.

- Captain Viola B. McConnell successfully evacuates more than 600 Americans out of Korea in 1950.

- Darlene Iskra becomes the first woman to command a ship in the US Navy in 1991.

- Michelle Howard is the first woman in the US Navy to become a four-star admiral.

- Kristen Griest and Shaye Haver become the first women to graduate from Army Ranger School.

WOMEN IN WAR

Women have played an important role during wartime, both on the home front and in the war zone in vital medical and clerical positions. During World War I, women were allowed to enlist for the first time, starting with the navy. Approximately 11,000 women served as Navy yeoman (F). Approximately 300,000 women served the US military in World War II. During the Korean War, approximately 120,000 served. Approximately 11,000 women served in the Vietnam War. When the US military became all-volunteer in 1973, women had new opportunities to achieve higher ranks. Starting with the Persian Gulf War, more and more women were deployed as active-duty service people. The wars in Afghanistan and Iraq created new roles for women, who were increasingly involved on the ground working with civilians.

IMPACT ON SOCIETY

Women serving in nursing and other noncombat roles have performed essential wartime duties. They have also enabled millions of male soldiers to fight. Women in volunteer organizations such as the Red Cross have provided valuable wartime support and materials, such as bandages and other medical supplies, to millions of soldiers. Women in leadership positions in governmental agencies such as the NSA have developed crucial programs to maintain the security and integrity of American affairs.

QUOTE

"Let's take this step and let women keep proving what they have already proved before."
—*Author Kayla Williams on admitting women into combat roles*

Glossary

BATTALION
A large number of troops ready for battle.

BODY ARMOR
Protective plates worn to shield the chest, abdomen, groin, and sides from injury.

CASUALTY
A person who is injured, missing, or killed during a military campaign.

COMMUNISM
A political system in which the government controls the economy and owns all property.

CRYPTOGRAPHER
A person who makes codes or tries to break other people's codes.

ESPIONAGE
The practice of spying.

FIELD HOSPITAL
A temporary medical facility set up near a combat zone.

GUERILLA
Warfare carried out in irregular ways, such as using sabotage, staging surprise raids, or fighting using unusual methods.

IMPROVISED EXPLOSIVE DEVICE (IED)

A bomb made from improvised materials, such as nails, glass, or metal.

INFANTRY

A group of soldiers trained and armed to fight on foot.

PROPAGANDA

Information used to support a political group or point of view, or to persuade the audience to support their country's participation in a war.

RATION

To set limits on the amount of certain foods or materials a population can purchase during war or other conflicts.

RESERVES

Group of military personnel who remain on standby so they can be available to address military needs quickly.

TOTALITARIAN

A type of government that is centralized and dictatorial.

WEAPON OF MASS DESTRUCTION (WMD)

A chemical, biological, or radioactive weapon capable of causing widespread injury, death, or destruction.

Additional Resources

SELECTED BIBLIOGRAPHY

Cohn, Carol. *Women and Wars: Contested Histories, Uncertain Futures*. Cambridge, UK: Polity, 2013. Print.

Holmstedt, Kirsten. *Band of Sisters*. Mechanicsburg, PA: Stackpole, 2008. Print.

Lemmon, Gayle Tzemach. *Ashley's War*. New York: Harper, 2015. Print.

FURTHER READINGS

Altwood, Kathryn J. *Women Heroes of World War I*. Chicago: Chicago Review, 2014. Print.

Altwood, Kathryn J. *Women Heroes of World War II*. Chicago: Chicago Review, 2011. Print.

Asselin, Kristine Carlson. *Women in World War I*. Minneapolis: Abdo, 2016. Print.

WEBSITES

To learn more about Women's Lives in History, visit **booklinks.abdopublishing.com**. These links are routinely monitored and updated to provide the most current information available.

FOR MORE INFORMATION

For more information on this subject, contact or visit the following organizations:

National Women's History Museum
205 South Whiting Street, Suite 254
Alexandria, VA 22304
703-461-1920
https://www.nwhm.org/
This museum features research and exhibits on the social, cultural, economic, and political contributions of women to US and world history.

US Army Women's Museum
2100 A Avenue, Building 5219
Fort Lee, VA 23801
804-734-4327
http://www.armywomensmuseum.org/index.htm
This museum offers information about the service of army women from 1775 to present.

Source Notes

CHAPTER 1. FEMALES WHO FIGHT

1. "Rick Santorum: Women in Combat Could Create Compromising Situation because of Emotions." *Huffington Post*. Huffington Post, 10 Feb. 2012. Web. 4 Mar. 2016.

2. James Webb. "Women Can't Fight." *Washingtonian*. Washingtonian, 1 Nov. 1979. Web. 4 Mar. 2016.

3. "The Life of King Henry the Fifth." *The Complete Works of William Shakespeare*. MIT, n.d. Web. 4 Mar. 2016.

4. James Webb. "Women Can't Fight." *Washingtonian*. Washingtonian, 1 Nov. 1979. Web. 4 Mar. 2016.

5. "Lozen: A Gifted Warrior." *Biography*. A&E, 23 Nov. 2014. Web. 4 Mar. 2016.

6. Tucker Carlson. "Feminism's Latest Victory: The Right to Get Your Limbs Blown Off in War. Congratulations." *Twitter*. Twitter, 24 Jan. 2013. Web. 4 Mar. 2016.

CHAPTER 2. THE GREAT WAR

1. Kim Pilling. "Women Are 'Forgotten Victims of First World War.'" *Independent*. Independent, 9 Nov. 2010. Web. 4 Mar. 2016.

2. Peter Craddick-Adams. "Women at War: 'She-Soldiers' Through the Ages." *BBC*. BBC, 1 Mar. 2005. Web. 4 Mar. 2016.

3. "They Heard the Call of Duty: Civil War Nurses." *Army Heritage Center Foundation*. Army Heritage Center Foundation, n.d. Web. 4 Mar. 2016.

4. "Clara Barton." *Biography*. A&E, n.d. Web. 4 Mar. 2016.

5. Baroness Williams Crosby. "World War One: The Many Battles Faced by WWI's Nurses." *BBC News*. BBC, 2 Apr. 2014. Web. 4 Mar. 2016.

6. Peter Craddick-Adams. "Women at War: 'She-Soldiers' Through the Ages." *BBC*. BBC, 1 Mar. 2005. Web. 4 Mar. 2016.

7. Sarah Martin. "Women and WWI—Women at the Front: Been There, Done That." *First World War.com*. Michael Duffy, 22 Aug. 2009. Web. 4 Mar. 2016.

8. Sophie Platt. "Last Known Yeoman (F) Laid To Rest." *United States Navy*. United States Navy, 30 Mar. 2007. Web. 4 Mar. 2016.

9. "Resources." *Women in Military Service for America Memorial Foundation*. Women in Military Service for America Memorial, n.d. Web. 4 Mar. 2016.

10. Elizabeth M. Collins. "World War I's Hello Girls: Paving the Way for Women in the U.S. Army." *Soldiers Magazine*. Soldiers Magazine, Mar. 2014. Web. 5 Apr. 2016.

11. "Recognition for Purposes of VA Benefits." *Rutgers Law*. Rutgers Law, 2012. Web. 5 Apr. 2016.

CHAPTER 3. WOMEN IN WORLD WAR II

1. CNN Library. "World War II Fast Facts." *CNN*. CNN, 31 July 2015. Web. 5 Apr. 2016.

2. "American Women in World War II." *History.com*. A&E, 2010. Web. 4 Mar. 2016.

3. Ibid.

4. Ibid.

5. "Women in the US Coast Guard." *United States Coast Guard*. US Department of Homeland Security, n.d. Web. 4 Mar. 2016.

6. "American Women in World War II." *History.com*. A&E, 2010. Web. 4 Mar. 2016.

7. "Resources." *Women in Military Service for America Memorial Foundation*. Women in Military Service for America Memorial, n.d. Web. 4 Mar. 2016.

8. Ibid.

9. "The Army Nurse Corps." *Army Nurse Corps*. US Army Center of Military History, 3 Oct. 2003. Web. 4 Mar. 2016.

10. "WWI and WWII US Navy Nurse Corps." *Armed Forces History Museum*. Armed Forces History Museum, 31 May 2012. Web. 4 Mar. 2016.

11. "Oveta Culp Hobby." *Army Woman's Museum*. Army Woman's Museum, n.d. Web. 4 Mar. 2016.

12. "The Army Nurse Corps." *Army Nurse Corps*. US Army Center of Military History, 3 Oct. 2003. Web. 4 Mar. 2016.

13. Ibid.

CHAPTER 4. WOMEN GAME CHANGERS

1. "Cold War History." *History.com*. A&E, 2009. Web. 4 Mar. 2016.

2. Robert W. Pringle. "KGB." *Encyclopedia Britannica*. Encyclopedia Britannica, 2016. Web. 4 Mar. 2016.

CHAPTER 5. WOMEN IN THE KOREAN WAR

1. Evelyn Monahan. *A Few Good Women*. New York: Anchor, 2010. 249. Print.

2. "Women in the Military in the Korean War." *Korean War Educator*. Korean War Educator, 21 Aug. 2015. Web. 4 Mar. 2016.

3. Ibid.

4. " Focus on the Korean War." *Women in Military Service for America Memorial Foundation*. Women in Military Service for America Memorial, n.d. Web. 4 Mar. 2016.

5. Laurie Weinstein. *Gender Camouflage*. New York: NYU, 1999. 21. Print.

6. "Executive Order 9981." *Women in Military Service for America Memorial Foundation*. Women in Military Service for America Memorial, n.d. Web. 4 Mar. 2016.

7. Judith Bellafaire. "Volunteering for Risk." *Women in Military Service for America Memorial Foundation*. Women in Military Service for America Memorial, n.d. Web. 4 Mar. 2016.

8. "Women in the Military in the Korean War." *Korean War Educator*. Korean War Educator, 21 Aug. 2015. Web. 4 Mar. 2016.

9. "Eras: 1950s." *Women in Military Service for America Memorial Foundation*. Women in Military Service for America Memorial, n.d. Web. 4 Mar. 2016.

10. Ibid.

11. "Korean War." *History.com*. A&E, 2009. Web. 4 Mar. 2016.

CHAPTER 6. WOMEN IN THE VIETNAM WAR

1. Meg Jones. "Legendary War Photographer Dickey Chapelle Back in Focus." *Journal Sentinel*. Journal Sentinel, 17 Oct. 2012. Web. 4 Mar. 2016.

2. "History Archive." *Women in Military Service for America Memorial Foundation*. Women in Military Service for America Memorial, n.d. Web. 4 Mar. 2016.

3. "Vietnam War History." *History.com*. A&E, 2009. Web. 4 Mar. 2016.

4. "Women in the Vietnam War." *History.com*. A&E, 2011. Web. 4 Mar. 2016.

5. Jeanne Holm and Sarah P. Wells. "Air Force Women in the Vietnam War." *Vietnam Women's Memorial*. Vietnam Women's Memorial, n.d. Web. 4 Mar. 2016.

6. Ibach Gallagher. "Memories of Navy Nursing." *Vietnam Women's Memorial*. Vietnam Women's Memorial, 10 Oct. 2015. Web. 4 Mar. 2016.

7. "Eras: 1960s." *Women in Military Service for America Memorial Foundation*. Women in Military Service for America Memorial, n.d. Web. 4 Mar. 2016.

Source Notes Continued

8. "Military Awards." *Army Publishing Directorate*. US Army, 25 June 2015. Web. 4 Mar. 2016.

9. Joyce Hoffman. "On Their Own: Female Correspondents in Vietnam." *Old Dominion University*. Old Dominion University, n.d. Web. 4 Mar. 2016.

10. "Women in the Vietnam War." *History.com*. A&E, 2011. Web. 4 Mar. 2016.

11. "American Civilian and Military Women Who Died in the Vietnam War (1959–1975). *Vietnam Women's Memorial*. Vietnam Women's Memorial, 29 Nov. 2012. Web. 4 Mar. 2016.

12. Kelly Schloesser. "The First Women of West Point." *US Army*. US Army, 27 Oct. 2010. Web. 4 Mar. 2016.

CHAPTER 7. WOMEN IN THE GULF WAR

1. "Highlights in the History of Military Women." *Women in Military Service for America Memorial Foundation*. Women in Military Service for America Memorial, n.d. Web. 4 Mar. 2016.

2. "USS *Opportune* Is Opportunity and Challenge for the Skipper, Darlene Iskra." *Baltimore Sun*. Baltimore Sun, 2 Nov. 1992. Web. 4 Mar. 2016.

3. Ibid.

4. "Persian Gulf War." *Women in Military Service for America Memorial Foundation*. Women in Military Service for America Memorial, n.d. Web. 4 Mar. 2016.

5. Maureen Murdoch, Arlene Bradley, Susan H. Mather, Robert E. Klein, Carole L. Turner, and Elizabeth M. Yano. "Women and War: What Physicians Should Know." *Journal of General Internal Medicine*. Blackwell Science, Mar. 2006. Web. 4 Mar. 2016.

6. Jon Nordheimer. "Women's Role in Combat: The War Resumes." *New York Times*. New York Times, 26 May 1991. Web. 4 Mar. 2016.

7. "36 Women Pregnant Aboard a Navy Ship That Served in Gulf." *New York Times*. New York Times, 30 Apr. 1991. Web. 4 Mar. 2016.

8. "24 Army Women Assaulted, Raped during Gulf War." *Sun Sentinel*. Sun Sentinel, 21 July 1992. Web. 4 Mar. 2016.

9. "Historical Frequently Asked Questions." *Women in Military Service for America Memorial Foundation*. Women in Military Service for America Memorial, n.d. Web. 4 Mar. 2016.

10. Erick Trickey. "Rhonda Cornum Biography." *Encyclopedia of World Biography*. Encyclopedia of World Biography, n.d. Web. 4 Mar. 2016.

11. "Don't Ask, Don't Tell (DADT)". *Encyclopedia Britannica*. Encyclopedia Britannica, 2016. Web. 4 Mar. 2016.

CHAPTER 8. WOMEN IN AFGHANISTAN AND IRAQ

1. Steve Hendrix. "F-16 Pilot Was Ready to Give Her Life on Sept. 11." *Washington Post*. Washington Post, 8 Sept. 2011. Web. 4 Mar. 2016.

2. Thomas E. Ricks. "Ashley's War." *Foreign Policy*. Foreign Policy, 21 Apr. 2015. Web. 4 Mar. 2016.

3. "Women in Combat: Some Lessons from the Israel Defense Forces." *NPR*. NPR, 19 May 2013. Web. 4 Mar. 2016.

4. "Memorandum for Secretaries of the Military Departments Acting under Secretary of Defense for Personnel and Readiness Chiefs of the Military Services." *Time Military*. Time, 24 Jan. 2013. Web. 4 Mar. 2016.

5. Mark Thompson. "Women in Combat." *Time*. Time, 25 Jan. 2013. Web. 4 Mar. 2016.

6. Thomas James Brennan. "Women in Combat? Some Marines React." *New York Times*. New York Times, 29 Jan. 2013. Web. 4 Mar. 2016.

7. Ibid.

8. Chelsea J. Carter and Steve Almasy. "Former Troops Say Time Has Come for Women in Combat Units." *CNN*. CNN, 24 Jan. 2015. Web. 4 Mar. 2016.

9. "Valor Knows No Gender." *NBC News*. NBC News, 24 Jan. 2015. Web. 4 Mar. 2016.

10. Chelsea J. Carter and Steve Almasy. "Former Troops Say Time Has Come for Women in Combat Units." *CNN*. CNN, 24 Jan. 2015. Web. 4 Mar. 2016.

11. Elspeth Reeve. "The Truth about Little Women Carrying Big Wounded Men in Combat." *The Wire*. Atlantic, 28 Jan. 2013. Web. 4 Mar. 2016.

12. Bryant Jordan. "Heavy Loads Could Burden Women's Infantry Role." *Military.com*. Military.com, 10 Apr. 2013. 4 Mar. 2016.

13. Elspeth Reeve. "The Truth about Little Women Carrying Big Wounded Men in Combat." *The Wire*. Atlantic, 28 Jan. 2013. Web. 4 Mar. 2016.

14. Robert J. Ehrlich. "Soldier's Load and Combat Readiness."*GlobalSecurity.org*. GlobalSecurity.org, n.d. Web. 4 Mar. 2016.

15. Ibid.

16. Kimberly Hefling. "US Army Rethinking How It Outfits Women." *Philly.com*. Philly.com, 1 May 2011. Web. 4 Mar. 2016.

17. Jeff Ward-Bailey. "How the Military Is Designing New Tactical Gear for Female Soldiers." *Christian Science Monitor*. Christian Science Monitor, 7 Dec. 2015. Web. 4 Mar. 2016.

CHAPTER 9. WOMEN IN FUTURE WARS

1. "Special Report: Women's History Month 2015." *Defense. gov*. US Department of Defense, Feb. 2015. Web. 4 Mar. 2016.

2. "By the Numbers: Women in the US Military." *CNN*. CNN, 24 Jan. 2013. Web. 4 Mar. 2016.

3. John P. Rafferty. "Michelle J. Howard." *Encyclopedia Britannica*. Encyclopedia Britannica, n.d. Web. 4 Mar. 2016.

4. "Airborne and Ranger Training Brigade." *US Army*. US Army, 3 Mar. 2016. Web. 4 Mar. 2016.

5. Alex Johnson and Lauren Prince. "Two Women Make History by Passing Army's Elite Ranger School." *NBC News*. NBC News, 18 Aug. 2015. Web. 4 Mar. 2016.

6. Elisabeth Braw. "Both Sexes Called to Arms as Norway Conscripts Girls." 3 Mar. 2015. Web. 4 Mar. 2016.

7. "Sexual Assault and Sexual Harassment in the US Military." *RAND*. RAND Corporation, 2014. Web. 4 Mar. 2016.

8. "Report Details Extra Problems Women Face in Military Careers." *CNN*. CNN, 16 Oct. 2009. Web. 4 Mar. 2016.

9. Stephen Losey. "Gender Neutral Standards Opening Combat Jobs to Women." *Air Force Times*. Air Force Times, 29 June 2015. Web. 4 Mar. 2016.

10. Chelsea J. Carter and Steve Almasy. "Former Troops Say Time Has Come for Women in Combat Units." *CNN*. CNN, 24 Jan. 2013. Web. 4 Mar. 2016.

11. Eileen Patten and Kim Parker. "Women in the US Military: Growing Share, Distinctive Profile." *Pew Research Center*. Pew Research Center, Dec. 2011. Web. 4 Mar. 2016.

12. Ibid.

13. Ibid.

14. "Special Report: Women's History Month 2015." *Defense.gov*. US Department of Defense, Feb. 2015. Web. 4 Mar. 2016.

Index

About the Author

Rebecca Rissman is a nonfiction author and editor. She has written more than 200 books about history, science, and art. Her book *Shapes in Sports* earned a starred review from *Booklist*, and her Animal Spikes and Spines series received *Learning Magazine*'s 2013 Teachers' Choice for Children's Books. She lives in Chicago, Illinois, with her husband and two daughters. She enjoys hiking, yoga, and cooking.